THIS BOOK IS THE PROPERTY OF:

Elkhart Baptist
Christian School

First Baptist Church
2626 Prairie
Elkhart, IN 46517

The fact that this volume appears in our library does not mean that the Elkhart Baptist Christian School necessarily endorses everything it says about morals, philosophy, theology or science. The position of the school is that these things must be interpreted in the light of the Scriptures. The Bible gives us our standards in all areas of life.

MUSHROOMS

THE EARTH'S GARDEN

Jason Cooper

Rourke Enterprises, Inc.
Vero Beach, Florida 32964

© 1991 Rourke Enterprises, Inc.

All rights reserved. No part of this book may be reproduced or utilized in any form or by any means, electronic or mechanical including photocopying, recording or by any information storage and retrieval system without permission in writing from the publisher.

PHOTO CREDITS

All Photographs © Lynn M. Stone

LIBRARY OF CONGRESS
Library of Congress Cataloging-in-Publication Data
Cooper, Jason, 1942-
   Mushrooms / by Jason Cooper.
    p. cm. — (The Earth's garden)
   Includes index.
   Summary: An introduction to the characteristics of mushrooms, how and where they grow, the different species, and their uses.
   ISBN 0-86592-623-9
   1. Mushrooms—Juvenile literature. [1. Mushrooms.] I. Title. II. Series: Cooper, Jason, 1942-   Earth's garden.
QK617.C75   1991
589.2'22—dc20   91-7142
                            CIP
                            AC

TABLE OF CONTENTS

Mushrooms	5
Mushroom Parts	6
New Mushrooms	9
Mushroom Homes	11
Kinds of Mushrooms	14
Funguses	16
Mushrooms Throughout the Year	19
Poisonous Mushrooms	20
Mushrooms and People	22
Glossary	23
Index	24

MUSHROOMS

Mushrooms are common, colorful, and valuable **funguses.** The best-known mushrooms look like they are wearing a cap or carrying an umbrella.

Until recent years the mushroom was called a plant. Mushrooms are now grouped with other funguses in a separate kingdom of living things.

Plants have chlorophyll, a green substance that helps them produce food. Mushrooms have no chlorophyll. They survive by taking food from living or dead plants.

Typical mushrooms carry an umbrella

MUSHROOM PARTS

A mushroom has two basic parts—the body and the **mycelium.** The colorful, fleshy part is the main body of the mushroom. Like a flower, this part of the mushroom lives only a short time.

The body of many mushrooms has a cap and a stalk. The stalk stands like a little post under the cap.

The mycelium is a web of threads under the stalk. It is hidden in wood, roots, soft plants, or rotting matter.

Mushroom cap and stalk

NEW MUSHROOMS

A mushroom produces millions of tiny **spores.** Light as dust, the spores travel with the wind. In the right place, a spore will make a new mycelium. The mycelium part of the mushroom feeds it and helps anchor it.

The body of the mushroom—the part we often think is the entire mushroom—dies rather quickly. The mycelium, however, may live for several years and send up several mushroom stalks and caps.

Underside of Collybia *mushroom cap*

MUSHROOM HOMES

Mushrooms usually live in grassy areas or forests.

Several kinds, or **species,** of mushrooms live on the dead parts of plants. Look for them on old leaves, pine needles, and logs.

Some mushrooms attack living plants. These mushrooms are **parasites.** Parasites live on or in another living thing and cause damage to it.

Other mushrooms live in such a way that they actually help tree roots. In turn, the mushrooms take food from the roots without harming them.

Pholiota *mushrooms growing on a log*

Lepiota *mushrooms in rich soil*

Puffball fungus is a cousin of mushrooms

KINDS OF MUSHROOMS

Nearly 3,000 species of mushrooms live in North America. They differ in size, color, shape, smell, taste, and touch. Some, for instance, are dry and others are slippery as seals.

Mushrooms also differ in their choice of places to grow. Certain kinds will grow only on trees.

Many mushrooms have unusual shapes. Coral mushrooms look like branches of the coral animals that grow in the ocean.

Coral mushroom (Clavaria) *resembles ocean coral*

FUNGUSES

Mushrooms and other funguses are somewhat like plants. But funguses, remember, can't make their own food. Plants can. Funguses live by taking food from plants and animals, dead or alive.

Funguses can be helpful or harmful. Athlete's foot, a common human skin disease, and some other diseases are caused by funguses. Some funguses help in making cheese and penicillin, an important medicine.

Shelf fungus, another mushroom cousin, growing on spruce tree

MUSHROOMS THROUGHOUT THE YEAR

In one place or another, mushrooms grow throughout the year. One mushroom is commonly known as "winter mushroom" because it grows during cold weather. Like flowers, each species of mushroom usually sprouts at roughly the same time each year.

Mushrooms usually appear in the greatest numbers during a wet autumn. A warm, wet spring also means a large mushroom crop.

A mushroom hunter in a damp forest may find dozens of different mushroom kinds.

Winter mushrooms (Collybia) *in late November*

POISONOUS MUSHROOMS

Mushroom hunters are extremely careful. They know that some mushrooms are tasty and good to eat. They know, too, that some kinds of mushrooms are bitter and even poisonous.

If eaten, poisonous mushrooms will make a person ill or even cause death. The problem is that the kinds of mushrooms are difficult to tell apart. Some of the most tasty mushrooms have deadly cousins that look like them.

Poisonous mushrooms are sometimes called toadstools, but a toadstool can be any capped mushroom.

Toad perched on "toadstool"

MUSHROOMS AND PEOPLE

For hundreds of years, mushrooms have been food for people. Today they are used in sauces, salads, omelettes, and pizzas.

Most of the mushrooms eaten in North America are raised on mushroom farms. Both the canned and fresh mushrooms for sale in markets are grown on farms.

Gathering wild mushrooms is fun if you can pick out the mushrooms that are safe. Never eat a wild mushroom until you are sure it is harmless.

Glossary

fungus (FUN gus) — a kingdom of living things that includes mushrooms

mycelium (my SEE lee um) — an often-hidden mass of living, threadlike structures that produce a mushroom body (stalk and cap)

parasite (PAIR uh site) — a plant (or animal) that lives on or in another plant or animal and harms it

species (SPEE sheez) — within a group of closely related living things, one certain kind, such as a *shaggy mane* mushroom

spore (SPORE) — a usually tiny particle produced by mushrooms and from which a new mushroom can grow

INDEX

athlete's foot 16
chlorophyll 5
forest 11, 19
funguses 5, 16
mushrooms
  canned 22
  cap of 5, 6, 9, 20
  coral 14
  homes of 11, 14, 19
  hunters of 19, 20, 22
  kinds of 11, 14, 20
  parts of 6
  poisonous 20
  shapes of 14
  stalk of 6, 9
  taste of 20
  uses of 22
  winter 19

mushroom farms 22
mycelium 6, 9
parasites 11
penicillin 16
plants 5, 11, 16
spores 9
toadstools 20
trees 14

DATE DUE			
FEB 0 6			
MAR 0 6			
NOV 1			
DE 1			
DE - 2 '02			
12/2			
JA 11 '08			
FE 5 '13			
AP 2 2 '13			

589.2(J) Cooper, Jason
Coo
    Mushrooms

GUMDROP BOOKS - Bethany, Missouri

Mushrooms /
589.2(J)Coo

Cooper, Jason,

WD

Elkhart Christian Academy

12071